Playing Safely

by Robin Nelson

Series consultants: Sonja Green, MD, and
Distinguished Professor Emerita Ann Nolte, PhD,
Department of Health Sciences, Illinois State University

Pull Ahead Books

Lerner Publications Company • Minneapolis

Lerner Publications Company
A division of Lerner Publishing Group
241 First Avenue North
Minneapolis, MN 55401 USA

Website address: www.lernerbooks.com

Words in **bold type** are explained in a glossary on page 31.

Library of Congress Cataloging-in-Publication Data

Nelson, Robin, 1971-
    Playing safely / by Robin Nelson ; Mrs. Kevin Scheibel
photography.
        p. cm. — (Pull ahead books)
    Includes index.
    ISBN-13: 978-0-8225-2632-2 (lib. bdg. : alk. paper)
    ISBN-10: 0-8225-2632-8 (lib. bdg. : alk. paper)
    1. Sports—Safety measures—Juvenile literature.
2. Accidents—Prevention—Juvenile literature. I. Scheibel,
Kevin, Mrs. II. Title. III. Series.
GV344.N45 2006
796'.028'9—dc22   2005007475

Manufactured in the United States of America
1 2 3 4 5 6 — JR — 11 10 09 08 07 06

Zack is getting ready to ride his bike to the pool with his mom. What do they need to do to stay safe?

Zack and his mom need to wear
helmets. A helmet protects your head
if you fall.

What rules keep you safe when you are on the street? Ride close to the **curb** and be aware of cars.

Use hand signals. Signals show others where you are going.

Obey all **traffic** signs when you ride
your bike or walk. Stop when you see
a stop sign.

Cross the street only at **crosswalks.**

Look all ways for cars before crossing the street. Walk your bike across busy **intersections**.

There is Zack's friend Cole. Cole is playing basketball. He waves to Zack. His ball rolls into the street. What should Cole do?

Stop! Never chase a ball into the street.
Get an adult to help you get your ball.

Zack's friend Sarah wears in-line skates to the pool. Sarah wears a helmet and knee and wrist **pads** for protection.

Zack and Sarah can't wait to get into the pool. But they know they need to follow water safety rules.

First, Zack and Sarah put on **sunscreen.** Sunscreen keeps your skin from burning.

Then they make sure there is a
lifeguard. The lifeguard watches the
pool to keep everyone safe.

Walk! Don't run around a pool. You could slip and fall very easily.

Play in **shallow** water. Your feet should be able to touch the bottom with your head out of the water.

It is only safe to dive in deep water.
Check that it is safe before diving.

Pay attention to signs around the pool. They tell you important rules to keep you safe.

Always swim with a buddy. A grown-up buddy is best.

Do you know what to do in a pool emergency?

Shout for help!

Here comes the lifeguard! If no
one comes, go find the lifeguard
or an adult.

The lifeguard is the best person to pull the swimmer to safety. The lifeguard has special training.

Take swimming lessons to learn more about what to do in an emergency. Swimming lessons teach you how to be safe in the water.

After lessons, Sarah's dad is waiting to drive her home. She says good-bye and buckles her seat belt. It helps her to be safe in the car.

Zack, Cole, and Sarah had a great day.
They remembered rules to keep them
safe. They stayed safe and had fun!

What Did You Learn?

- Wear a helmet and pads when skating or riding a bike. Use hand signals.

- Be careful around cars and on the street. Look all directions and obey traffic signs.

- Wear sunscreen.

- Don't run around the pool.

- Swim and play in shallow water.

- Don't swim without a lifeguard or an adult.

- It is important to know what to do in a pool emergency. Here are some things to remember:
  - call for help
  - push something that floats, like a life jacket, out to the swimmer
  - go get the lifeguard or an adult to help
  - don't get in the water with the swimmer.

- Buckle your seat belt.

Hand Signals

When you are riding your bike, you should use hand signals to show others where you are going. There are three signals. Always use your left hand.

■ Put your hand straight out if you are going to turn left.

■ Bend your hand up if you are going to turn right.

■ Bend your hand down if you are going to stop.

Books and Websites

Books

Boelts, Maribeth. *A Kid's Guide to Staying Safe around Water.* New York: PowerKids Press, 1997.

Leaney, Cindy. *Look Out!: A Story about Safety on Bicycles.* Vero Beach, FL: Rourke Publishing, 2003.

McGinty, Alice B. Staying Healthy: Personal Safety. New York: PowerKids Press, 1997.

Websites

The National Highway Safety Administration's Safety City
http://www.nhtsa.dot.gov/kids/

National Safe Kids Campaign
http://www.safekids.org

Pool Kids Safety Trivia
http://www.poolkidsusa.com/

Traffic Safety Kids Page
http://www.nysgtsc.state.ny.us/kids.htm

Glossary

crosswalks: marked paths for people crossing the street

curb: the edge of a road

helmets: hats that are worn to protect the head

intersections: places where two streets cross

lifeguard: a person who watches swimmers to keep them safe

pads: gear that protects your body if you fall

shallow: not deep

sunscreen: a lotion that stops sunburn

traffic: cars, trucks, and buses on streets

Index